Easy Origami 2

General Origami

Origami Symphony No. 1: The Elephant's Trumpet Call
DC Super Heroes Origami
Origami Worldwide
Teach Yourself Origami: Second Revised Edition
Storytime Origami
Origami Inside-Out: Third Edition
Christmas Origami: Second Edition

Animal Origami

Dogs in Origami
Perfect Pets Origami
Dragons and Other Fantastic Creatures in Origami
Bugs in Origami
Horses in Origami
Origami Birds
Origami Gone Wild
Dinosaur Origami
Origami Dinosaurs for Beginners
Prehistoric Origami: Dinosaurs and other Creatures: Third Edition
Mythological Creatures and the Chinese Zodiac Origami
Origami Under the Sea
Sea Creatures in Origami
Origami Sea Life: Third Edition
Bringing Origami to Life
Bugs and Birds in Origami
Origami Sculptures: Fourth Edition
African Animals in Origami: Third Edition
North American Animals in Origami: Third Edition

Geometric Origami

Origami Stars
Galaxy of Origami Stars: Second Edition
Origami and Math: Simple to Complex
Origami & Geometry
3D Origami Platonic Solids & More: Second Edition
3D Origami Diamonds
3D Origami Antidiamonds
3D Origami Pyramids
A Plethora of Polyhedra in Origami: Third Edition
Classic Polyhedra Origami
A Constellation of Origami Polyhedra
Origami Polyhedra Design

Dollar Bill Origami

Dollar Origami Treasures: Second Edition
Dollar Bill Animals in Origami: Second Revised Edition
Dollar Bill Origami
Easy Dollar Bill Origami

Simple Origami

Fun and Simple Origami: 101 Easy-to-Fold Projects: Second Edition
Super Simple Origami
Easy Dollar Bill Origami
Easy Origami Animals
Easy Origami Polar Animals
Easy Origami Ocean Animals
Easy Origami Woodland Animals
Easy Origami Jungle Animals
Meditative Origami

Introduction

Here is a collection of 36 simple, traditional projects. Clear step-by-step instructions make these fun and easy to fold. Subjects include hats, boats, boxes, birds, objects, and more. You can fold a yacht, tall sailboat, party hat, rose, parakeet, and the famous flapping bird.

This collection is perfect for children, new folders, and art teachers. More models include a fancy card, pagoda, navy cap, wild duck, dove, and candy dish. By learning to fold these traditional favorites, the folder can make a large variety of subjects.

The diagrams are drawn in the internationally approved Randlett–Yoshizawa style, which, you will find, is easy to follow once you have learned the basic folds. You can use any kind of square paper for these models, but the best results and most precise folding can be achieved using standard origami paper, which is colored on one side and white on the other. In these diagrams, the shading represents the colored side. Origami supplies are found at arts and crafts stores, or at Origami USA: www.origamiusa.org. Online sites such as OrigamiUSA will help you find local, national, and international groups practicing the art of origami around the world.

Please follow me on Instagram @montrollorigami to see posts of my origami.

Good Luck and Happy Folding!

John Montroll
www.johnmontroll.com

Easy Origami 2

ISBN-10: 1-877656-47-X
ISBN-13: 978-877656-47-7

Antroll Publishing Company

Contents

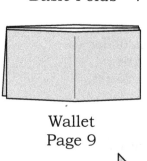

Wallet
Page 9

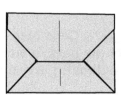

Envelope
Page 10

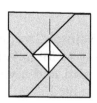

Fancy Card
Page 11

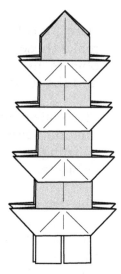

Pagoda
Page 14

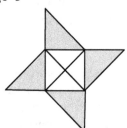

Four-Pointed Star
Page 12

Church
Page 13

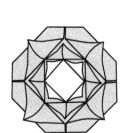

Fortune Teller
Page 16

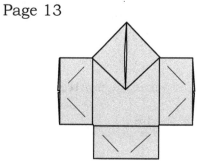

Rose
Page 17

Yakko-San
Page 18

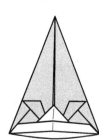

Party Hat
Page 19

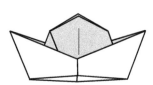

Cowboy Hat
Page 20

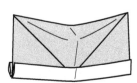

Navy Cap
Page 21

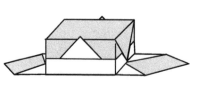

Officer's Hat
Page 22

Crown
Page 23

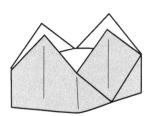

King's Crown
Page 24

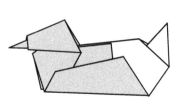

Wild Duck
Page 25

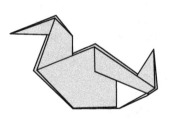

Waterfowl
Page 26

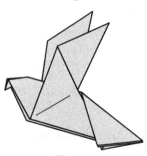

Dove
Page 27

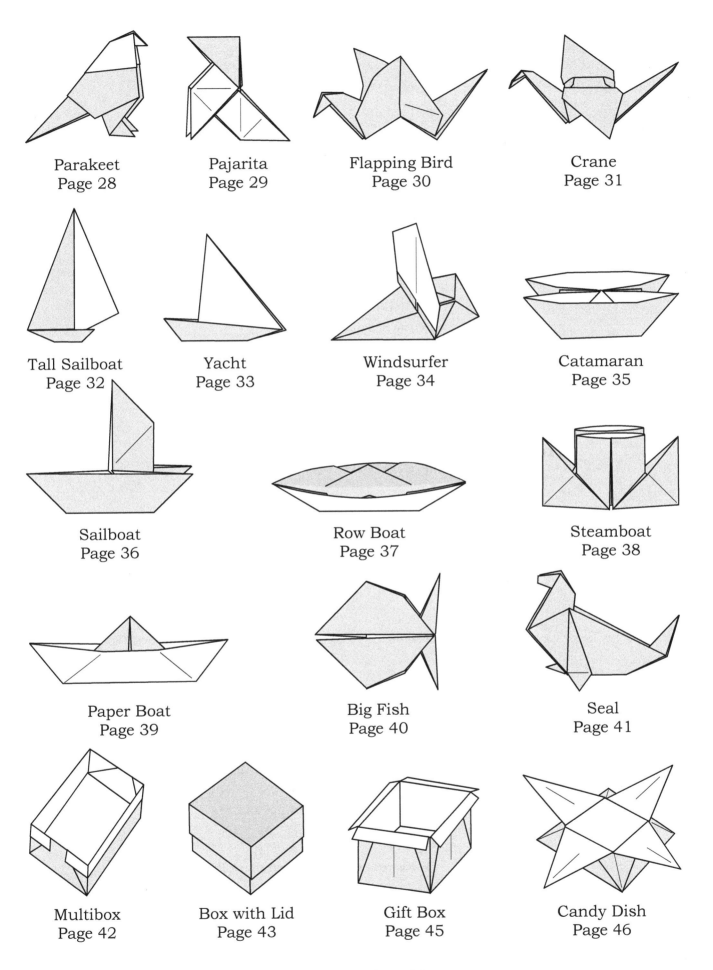

Parakeet
Page 28

Pajarita
Page 29

Flapping Bird
Page 30

Crane
Page 31

Tall Sailboat
Page 32

Yacht
Page 33

Windsurfer
Page 34

Catamaran
Page 35

Sailboat
Page 36

Row Boat
Page 37

Steamboat
Page 38

Paper Boat
Page 39

Big Fish
Page 40

Seal
Page 41

Multibox
Page 42

Box with Lid
Page 43

Gift Box
Page 45

Candy Dish
Page 46

Symbols

Lines

— — — — — — — —   Valley fold, fold in front.

—··—··—··—··—··—.   Mountain fold, fold behind.

————————————   Crease line.

·····················   X-ray or guide line.

Arrows

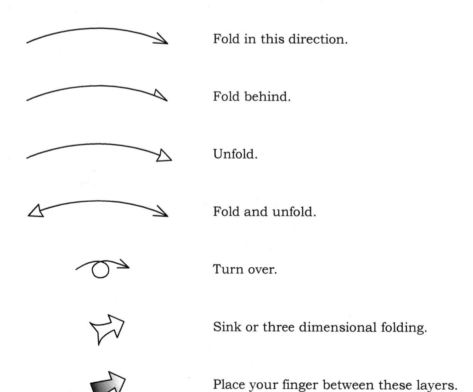

Fold in this direction.

Fold behind.

Unfold.

Fold and unfold.

Turn over.

Sink or three dimensional folding.

Place your finger between these layers.

Basic Folds

Squash Fold.

In a squash fold, some paper is opened and then made flat. The shaded arrow shows where to place your finger.

1

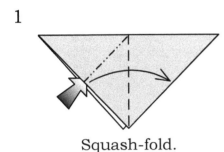

Squash-fold.

2

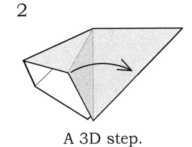

A 3D step.

3

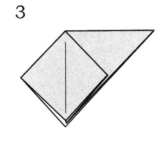

Petal Fold.

In a petal fold, one point is folded up while two opposite sides meet each other.

1

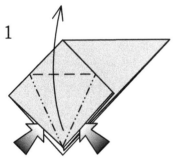

Petal-fold.

2

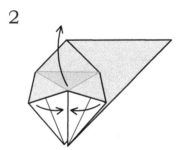

A 3D step.

3

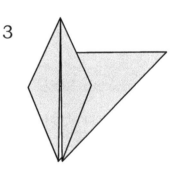

Inside Reverse Fold.

In an inside reverse fold, some paper is folded between layers. Here are two examples.

1

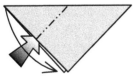

Reverse-fold.

2

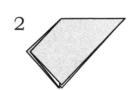

1

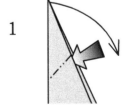

Reverse-fold.

2

Preliminary Fold.

The Preliminary Fold is the starting point for many models. The maneuver in step 3 occurs in many other models.

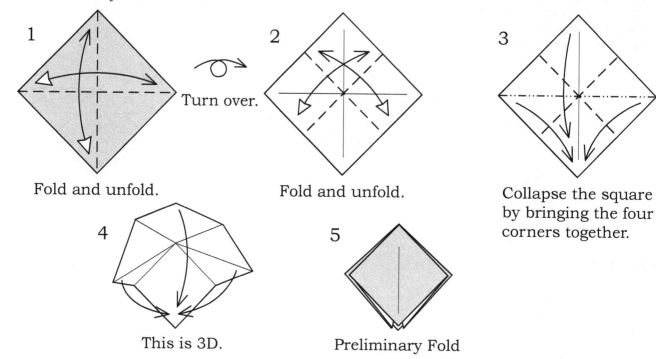

1 Fold and unfold.

Turn over.

2 Fold and unfold.

3 Collapse the square by bringing the four corners together.

4 This is 3D.

5 Preliminary Fold

Waterbomb Base.

The waterbomb base is named for the waterbomb balloon which is made from it.

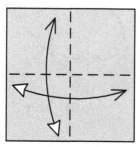

1 Fold and unfold.

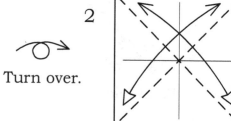

Turn over.

2 Fold and unfold.

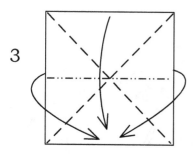

3 Collapse along the creases.

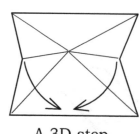

4 A 3D step.

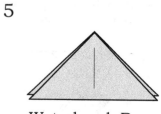

5 Waterbomb Base

Wallet

1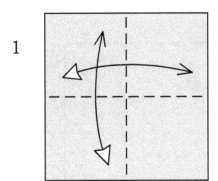

Fold and unfold.

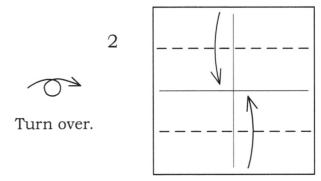

Turn over.

2

Fold to the center.

3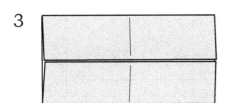

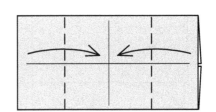

Turn over.

4

Fold to the center.

5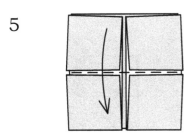

Fold in half.

6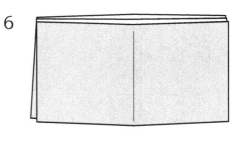

Wallet

Envelope

1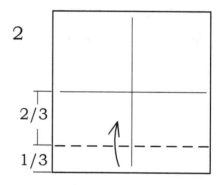

Fold and unfold.

2

2/3

1/3

Fold up one-third.

3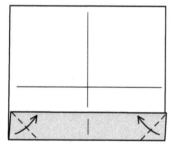

4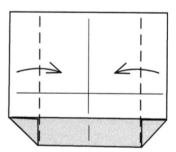

5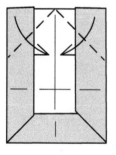

Fold to the center.

6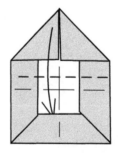

Tuck inside.

7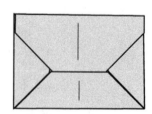

Envelope

Fancy Card

1

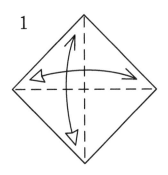

Fold and unfold.

2

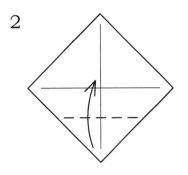

Fold above the center.

3

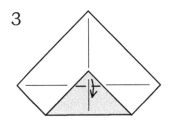

Fold along the
hidden crease.

4

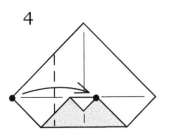

The dots
will meet.

5

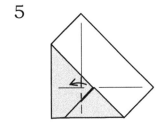

Fold along the
hidden crease.

6

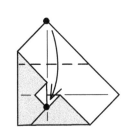

The dots
will meet.

7

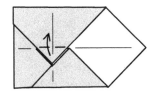

Fold along the
hidden crease.

8

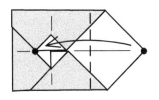

The dots
will meet.

9

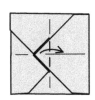

Fold along the
hidden crease.

10

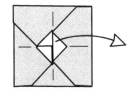

Unfold.

11

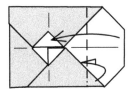

Reverse-fold.

12

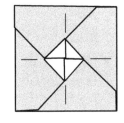

Fancy Card

Four-Pointed Star

1
Fold and unfold.

2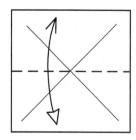
Fold and unfold.

3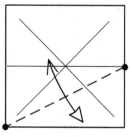
Fold and unfold.

4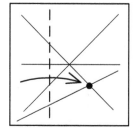
Fold to the dot.

5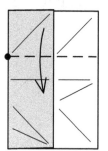

6
Pull out
the corner.

7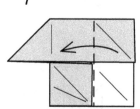

8
Pull out
the corner.

9

10
Pull out
the corner.

11
Pull out
the corner.

12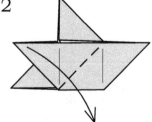

13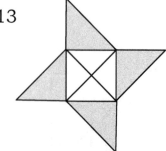

Four-Pointed
Star

Church

1
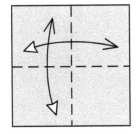
Fold and unfold.

2
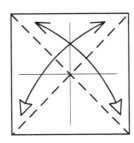
Fold and unfold.

3
Collapse along
the creases.

4

This is the
Waterbomb Base.
Fold the flap up.

5
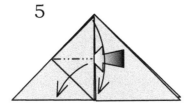
Squash-fold.

6

Repeat steps 4–5
on the right.

7
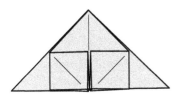
Repeat steps
4–6 behind.

8
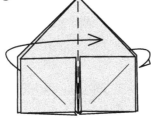
Fold to the right
and repeat behind.

9
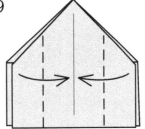
Fold the top layers
to the center.
Repeat behind.

10
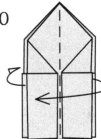
Fold to the left
and repeat
behind.

11
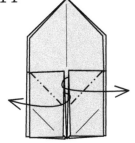
Make squash folds.

12
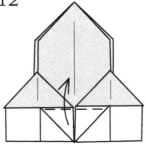
Fold up.

13
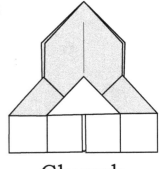
Church

Pagoda

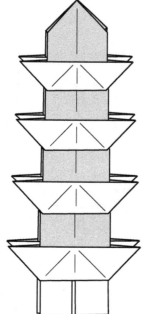

1

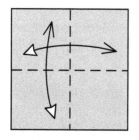

Fold and unfold.

2

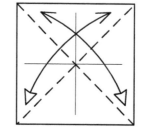

Fold and unfold.

3

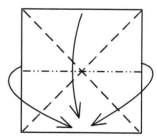

Collapse along
the creases.

4

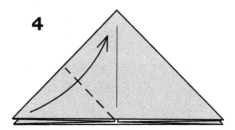

This is the Waterbomb
Base. Fold the flap up.

5

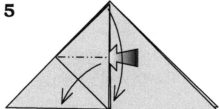

Squash-fold.

6

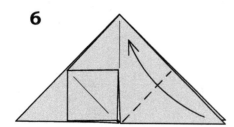

Repeat steps 4–5
on the right.

7

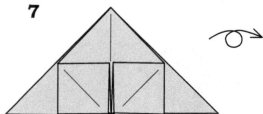

8

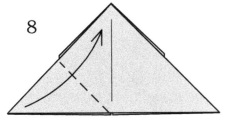

Repeat steps 4–6.

9

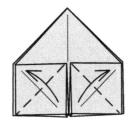

Fold up and
repeat behind.

10

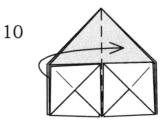

Fold to the right
and repeat behind.

11

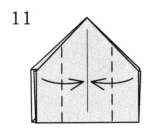

Fold the top layers
to the center.
Repeat behind.

12

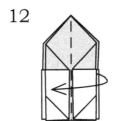

Fold to the left and
repeat behind.

13

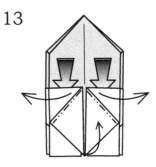

Spread the paper.
Repeat behind.

14

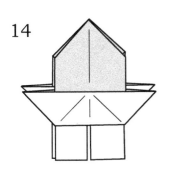

This is one unit. Fold
several in decreasing
sizes and stack them.

15

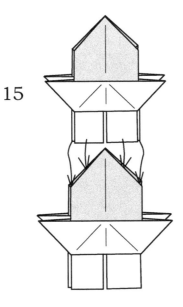

Attach the units.

16

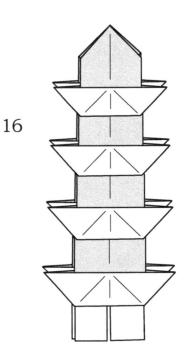

Pagoda

Fortune Teller

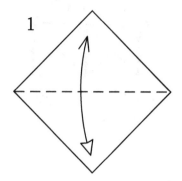

1

Fold and unfold.

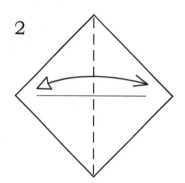

2

Fold and unfold.

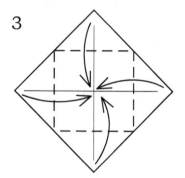

3

Fold the corners to the center.

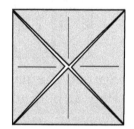

4

This is the Blintz Fold.

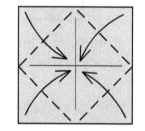

5

Fold to the center.

6

Fold in half.

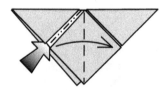

7

Squash-fold.

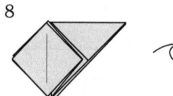

8

9

Squash-fold.

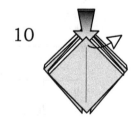

10

Spread the four corners.

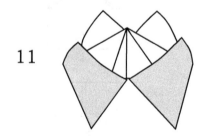

11

In England this is often used as a salt cellar, and in Japan as a candy dish.

Fortune Teller (or Cootie Catcher)

Rose

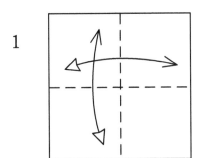

1

Fold and unfold.

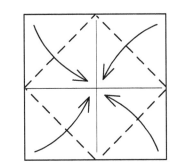

2

Fold to the center.

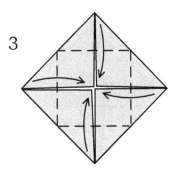

3

Fold to the center.

4

Fold to the center
(third time).

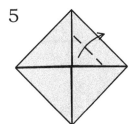

5

Fold the corner
beyond the edge.

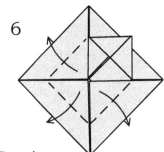

6

Continue
three times.

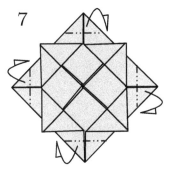

7

Fold the corners
behind.

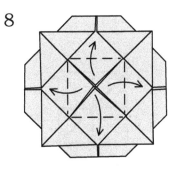

8

Fold the top
corners.

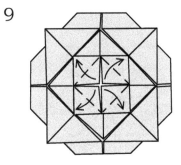

9

Fold the corners.

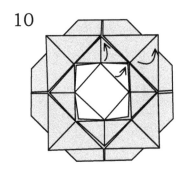

10

Curl all the petals.

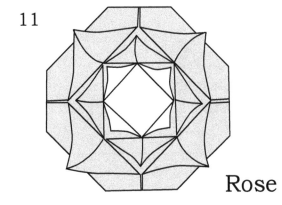

11

Rose

Yakko-San

1

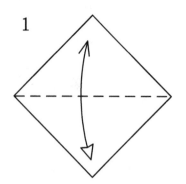

Fold and unfold.

2

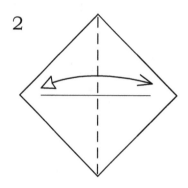

Fold and unfold.

3

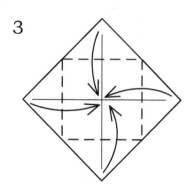

Fold the corners to the center.

4

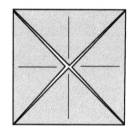

This is the Blintz Fold.

5

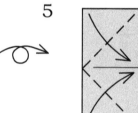

Fold to the center.

6

7

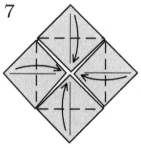

Fold to the center.

8

Turn over and rotate.

9

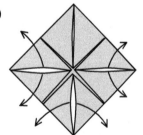

Open on three sides.

10

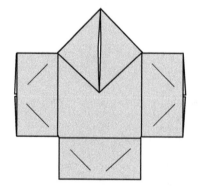

Yakko-San

Wrestler

Party Hat

1
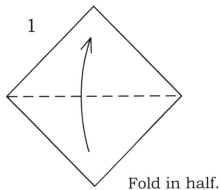
Fold in half.

2
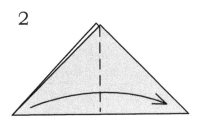
Fold in half.

3
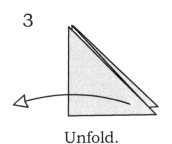
Unfold.

4
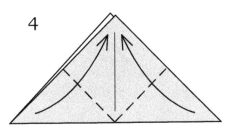
Fold the corners to the top.

5
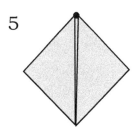
Turn over and
rotate the dot
to the bottom.

6

Fold to the center.

7
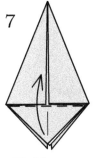
Fold one
layer up.

8
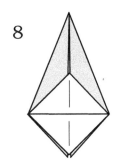

9
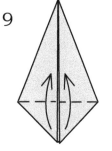
Fold the two
corners up.

10
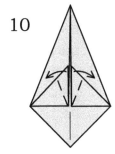
Fold the two
corners.

11
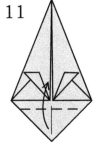
Fold up.

12
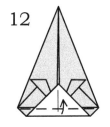
Fold a thin
strip up.

13
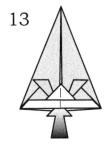
Open the hat.

14
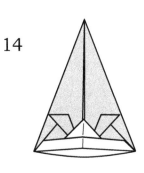
Party Hat

Cowboy Hat

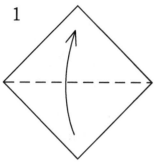

1

Fold in half.

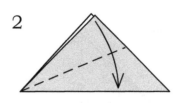

2

Fold the top
layer down.

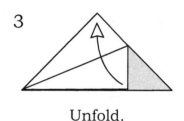

3

Unfold.

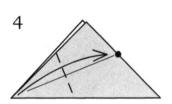

4

Fold the corner
to the dot.

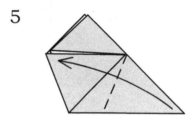

5

Fold the
other corner.

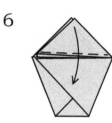

6

Fold the top
layer down.

7

Fold behind along
the mountain fold
line. Rotate the top
to the bottom.

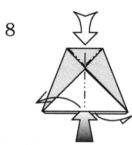

8

Place your finger inside to
open at the bottom. Push
in at the top. Make the
model 3D, then flatten.

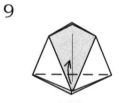

9

Fold up.
Repeat behind.

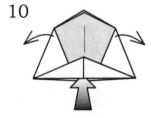

10

Spread on both sides
and open the hat.

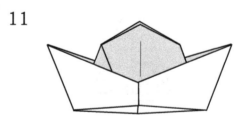

11

Cowboy Hat

Navy Hat

1
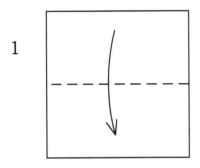
Fold in half.

2
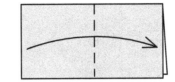
Fold in half.

3
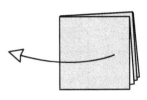
Unfold.

4
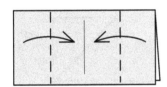
Fold to the center.

5
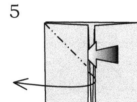
Squash-fold.

6
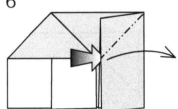
Squash-fold.

7
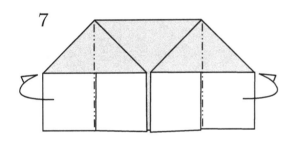
Fold behind.

8
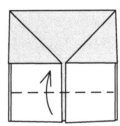
Fold up and
repeat behind.

9
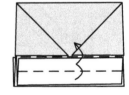
Repeat behind.

10

Push in at the top and
open at the bottom.

11
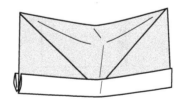
Navy Cap

Officer's Hat

1

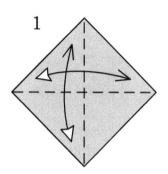

Fold and unfold.

2

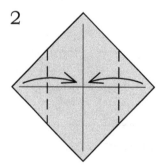

Fold two corners to the center.

3

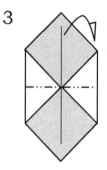

Fold behind.

4

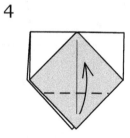

Fold up. The amount is not important. Repeat behind.

5

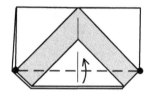

Fold up. Repeat behind.

6

Squash-fold.

7

8

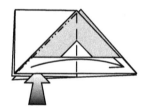

Squash-fold.

9

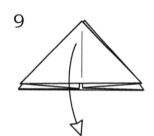

Fold the top layer down. Repeat behind.

10

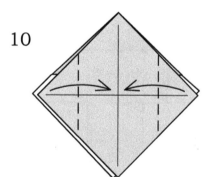

Fold to the center. Repeat behind.

11

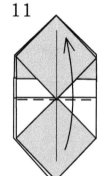

Fold up. Repeat behind.

12

Open and spread the hat.

13

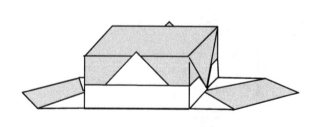

Officer's Hat

Crown

1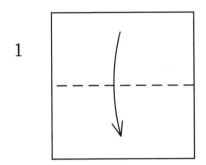

Fold in half.

2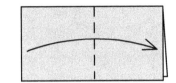

Fold in half.

3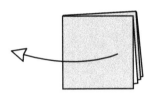

Unfold.

4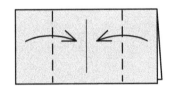

Fold to the center.

5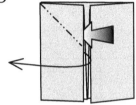

Squash-fold.

6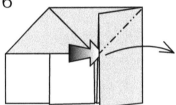

Squash-fold.

7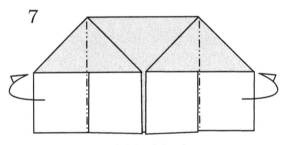

Fold behind.

8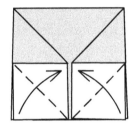

Repeat behind.

9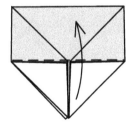

Repeat behind.

10

Push in at the top and open at the bottom.

11

Crown

King's Crown

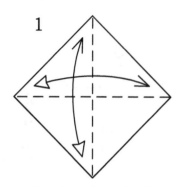

1

Fold and unfold.

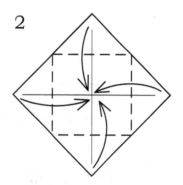

2

Fold the corners to the center.

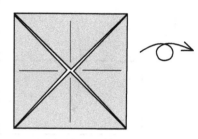

3

This is the Blintz Fold.

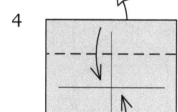

4

Fold to the center and swing out from behind.

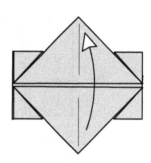

5

Lift up.

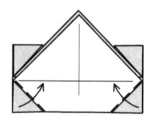

6

Fold up.

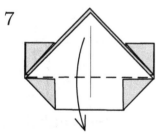

7

Fold along the crease.

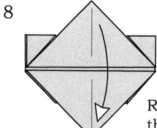

8

Repeat steps 5–7 in the other direction.

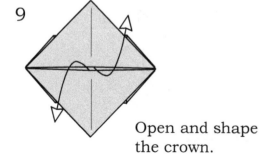

9

Open and shape the crown.

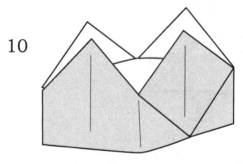

10

King's Crown

Wild Duck

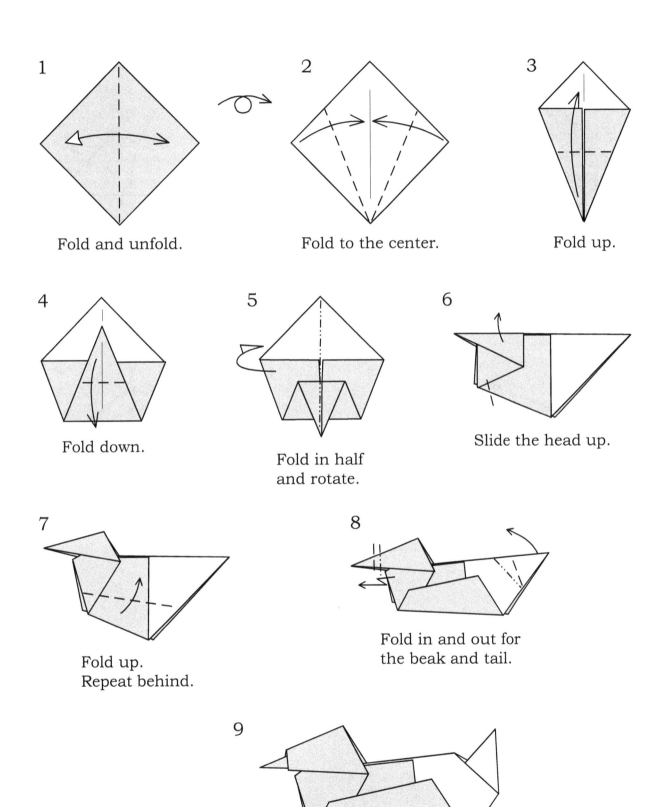

1 Fold and unfold.

2 Fold to the center.

3 Fold up.

4 Fold down.

5 Fold in half and rotate.

6 Slide the head up.

7 Fold up. Repeat behind.

8 Fold in and out for the beak and tail.

9

Wild Duck

Waterfowl

1

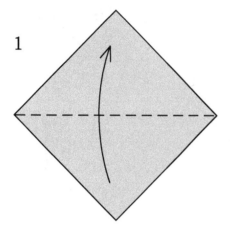

Fold in half.

2

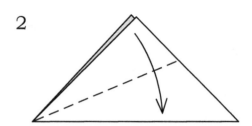

Fold to the bottom.
Repeat behind.

3

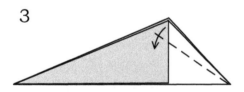

Repeat behind.

4

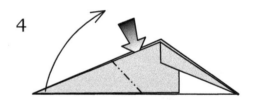

Place your finger
between the layers
for this reverse fold.

5

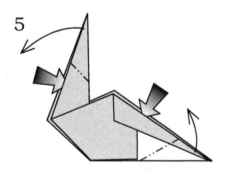

Reverse-fold the
head and tail.

6

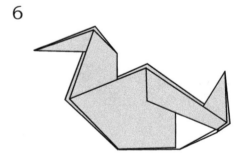

Waterfowl

Dove

1

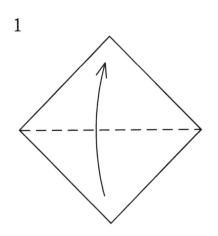

Fold in half.

2

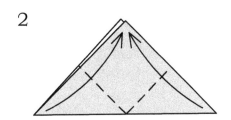

Fold the corners
up. Rotate 90°.

3

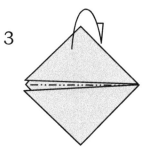

Fold behind.

4

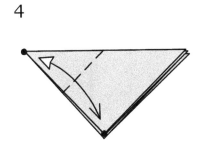

Fold all the layers
and unfold.

5

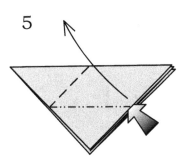

Squash-fold.
Repeat behind.

6

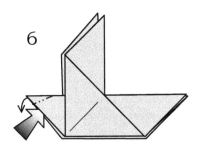

Reverse-fold
the beak.

7

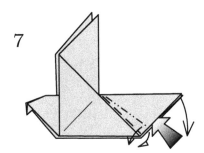

Place your finger
inside to bend the tail.

8

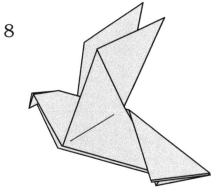

Dove

Parakeet

1

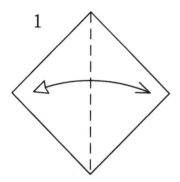

Fold and unfold.

2

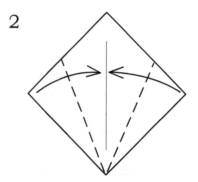

Fold to the center.

3

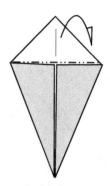

Fold behind.

4

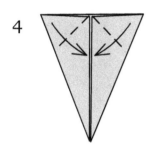

Fold to the center.

5

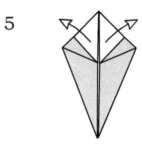

Unfold.

6

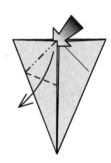

Squash-fold.

7

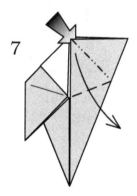

Squash-fold.

8

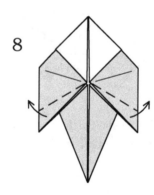

Fold up.

9

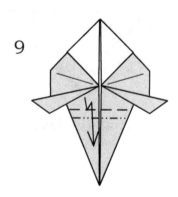

Fold back
and forth.

10

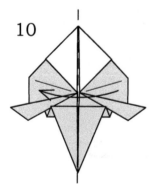

Fold in half
and rotate.

11

Reverse-fold
the beak.

12

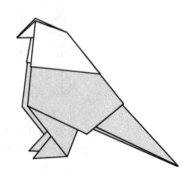

Parakeet

Pajarita

1

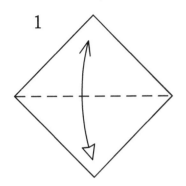

Fold and unfold.

2

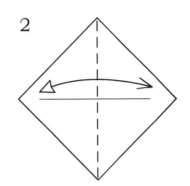

Fold and unfold.

3

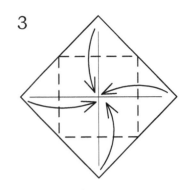

Fold the corners
to the center.

4

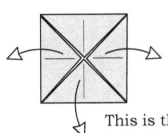

This is the Blintz
Fold. Unfold on
three sides.

5

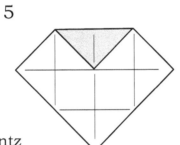

6

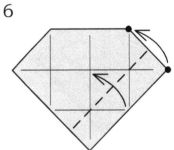

Fold to the dot.

7

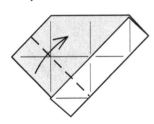

Fold on the left.

8

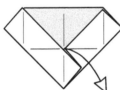

Pull out
the corner.

9

Fold to the
center.

10

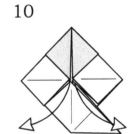

Pull out two
corners.

11

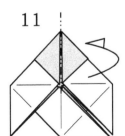

Fold in half.

12

Pull out
the corner.

13

Pajarita
"Little Bird"
in Spanish.

Flapping Bird

1

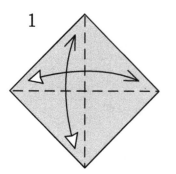

Fold and unfold.

2

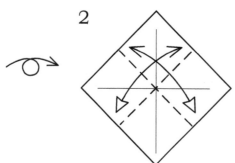

Fold and unfold.

3

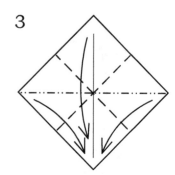

Fold along
the creases.

4

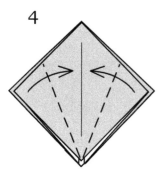

Kite-fold the
top layers and
repeat behind.

5

Fold all the layers
and unfold.

6

Unfold, repeat
behind.

7

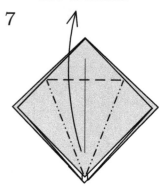

Petal-fold.

8

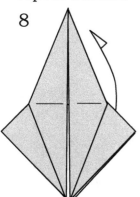

Petal-fold behind.

9

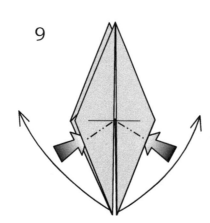

Make reverse folds.

10

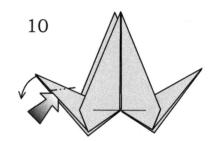

Reverse-fold.

11

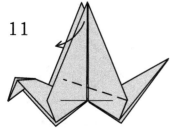

Fold the wing out.
Repeat behind.

12

Pull the tail back and
forth while holding at
the bottom of the neck
to flap the wings. The
white circles show
where to hold.

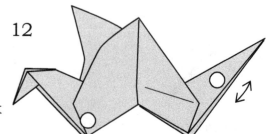

Flapping Bird

Crane

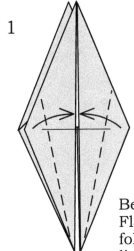

1

Begin with step 9 of the Flapping Bird. For this kite fold, fold close to the center line but not exactly on it. Repeat behind.

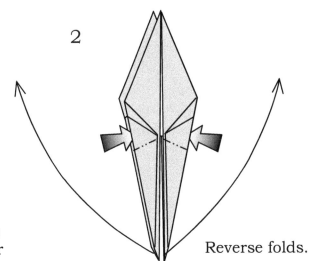

2

Reverse folds.

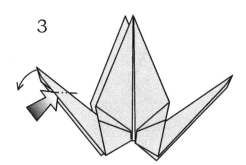

3

Reverse-fold.

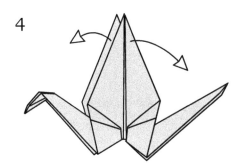

4

Pull the wings apart and let the body open.

5

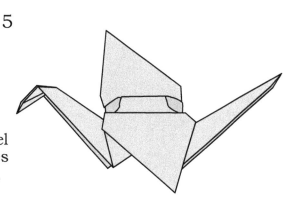

This is perhaps the most famous model in all of origami. The crane symbolizes peace and hope; a thousand cranes, often strung together, are folded for many occasions. Many Japanese children know this model. Being able to fold it is a milestone.

Crane

Tall Sailboat

1

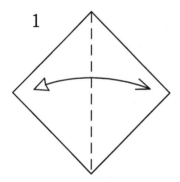

Fold and unfold.

2

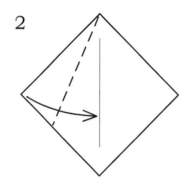

Fold to the center.

3

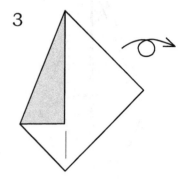

4

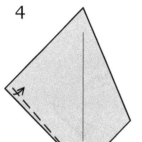

Fold a thin strip.

5

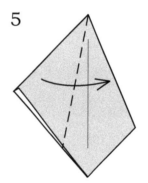

6

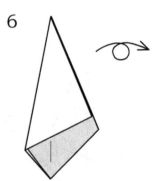

7

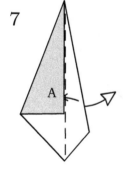

A

Fold under flap A
and swing out
from behind.

8

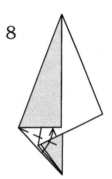

9

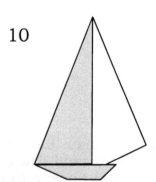

Fold behind.

10

Tall Sailboat

Yacht

1

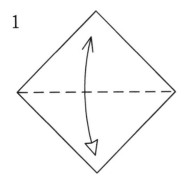

Fold and unfold.

2

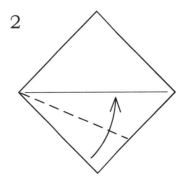

Fold to the center.

3

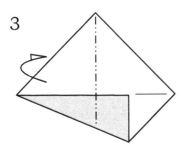

Fold in half
and behind.

4

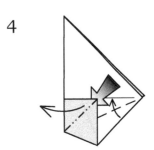

Squash-fold.

5

Fold all the
layers behind.

6

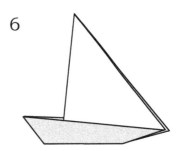

Yacht

Windsurfer

1

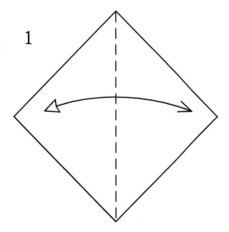

Fold and unfold.

2

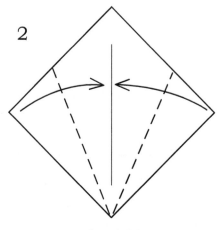

Kite-fold.

3

Fold in half.

4

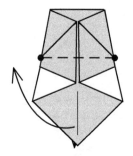

Fold to the center.

5

Fold straight up.

Blow to move
the windsurfer.

6

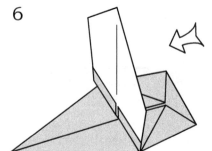

Windsurfer

Catamaran

 1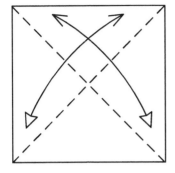

Fold and unfold.

2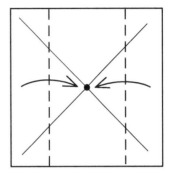

Fold to the center.

3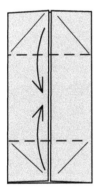

Fold to the center.

4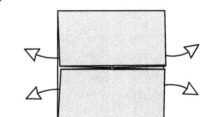

Pull out the corners.

5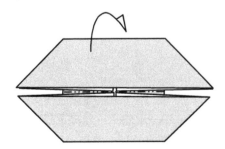

Fold behind.

6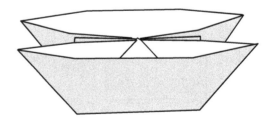

Catamaran

Sailboat

1
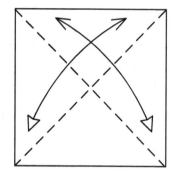

Fold and unfold.

2
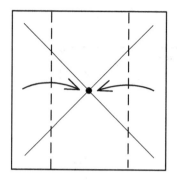

Fold to the center.

3
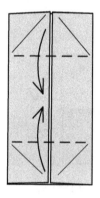

Fold to the center.

4
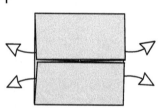

Pull out the corners.

5
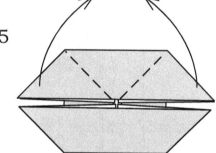

Fold up.

6
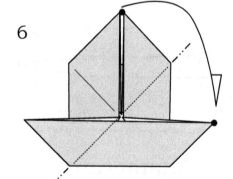

Fold behind so the dots meet.

7
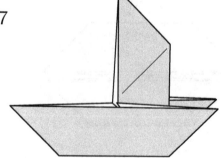

Sailboat

Row Boat

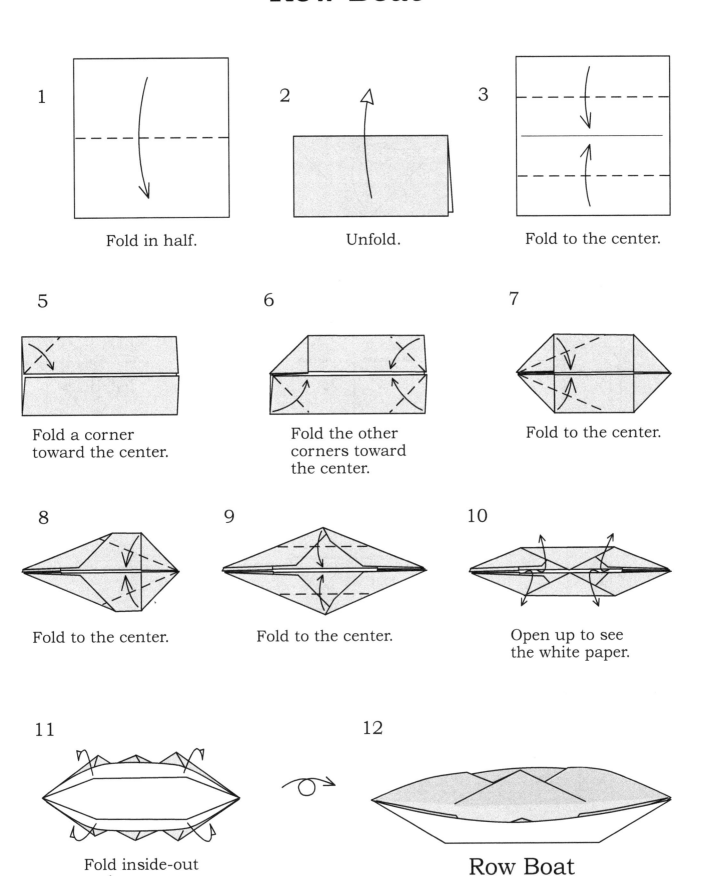

1 Fold in half.

2 Unfold.

3 Fold to the center.

5 Fold a corner toward the center.

6 Fold the other corners toward the center.

7 Fold to the center.

8 Fold to the center.

9 Fold to the center.

10 Open up to see the white paper.

11 Fold inside-out and turn over.

12 Row Boat

Steamboat

1

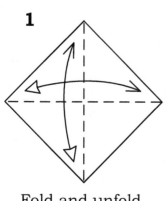

Fold and unfold.

2

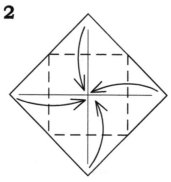

Fold the corners
to the center.

3

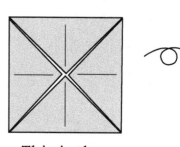

This is the
Blintz Fold.

4

Fold to the
center.

5

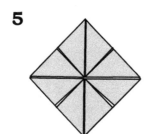

6

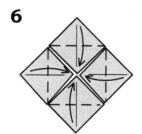

Fold to the
center.

7

Turn over
and rotate.

8

Open on
two sides.

9

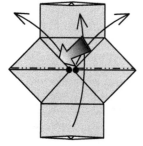

Fold in half and pop
out the two corners
with the dots.

10

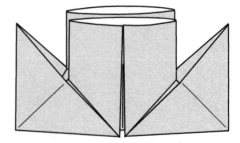

Steamboat

Paper Boat

This is a variation of the traditional boat from a rectangle.

1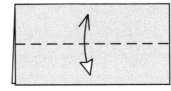

Fold in half.

2

Fold the top layer in half and unfold.

3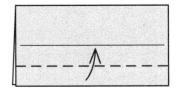

Fold the top layer to the crease. Repeat behind.

4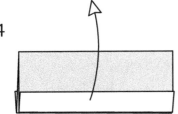

Unfold and rotate.

5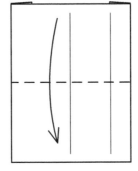

Fold in half.

6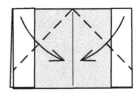

Fold to the center.

7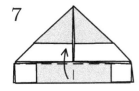

Fold the top layer up. Repeat behind.

8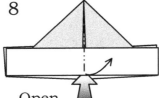

Open.

9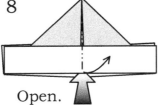

This is a 3D intermediate step. Continue and then flatten so the dots are on the left and right.

10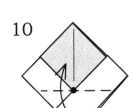

Fold up. Repeat behind.

11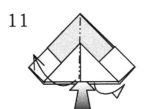

Open. This is the same as steps 8 and 9.

12

Fold up and spread on the left and right. Repeat behind.

13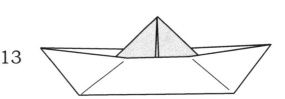

Paper Boat

Big Fish

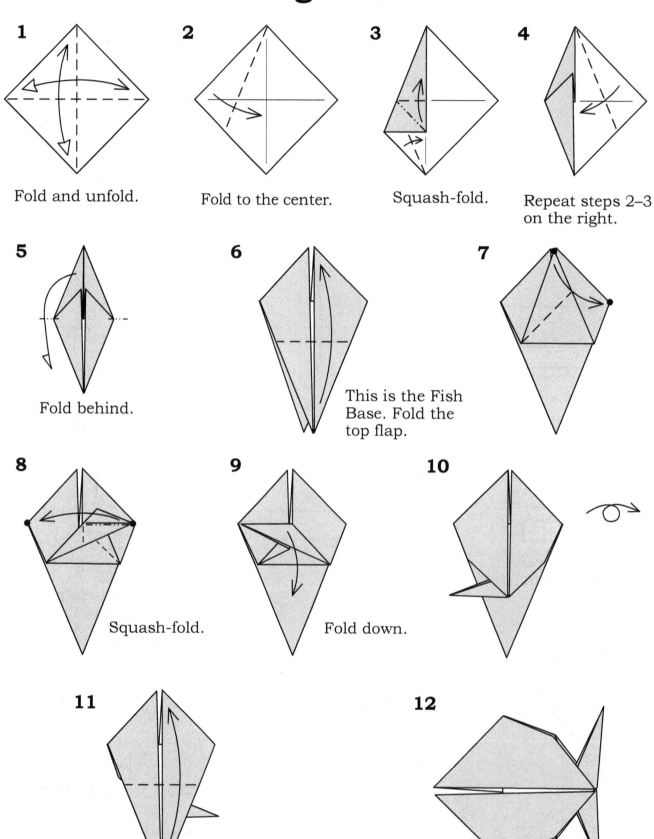

1 Fold and unfold.

2 Fold to the center.

3 Squash-fold.

4 Repeat steps 2–3 on the right.

5 Fold behind.

6 This is the Fish Base. Fold the top flap.

7

8 Squash-fold.

9 Fold down.

10

11 Repeat steps 6–10. Rotate.

12 **Big Fish**

Seal

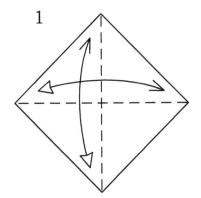

1

Fold and unfold.

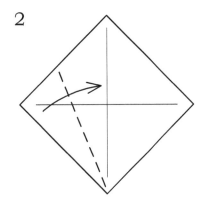

2

Fold to the center.

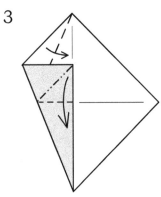

3

Squash-fold.

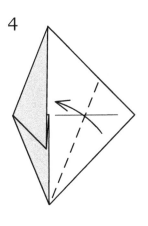

4

Repeat steps 2–3 on the right.

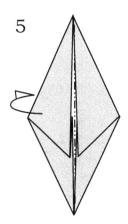

5

Fold in half and rotate.

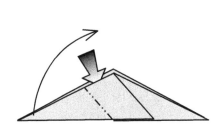

6

Reverse-fold.

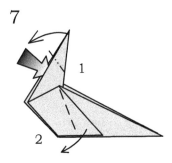

7

1. Reverse-fold.
2. Fold down and repeat behind.

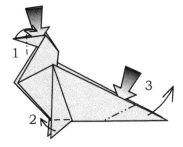

8

1. Reverse-fold.
2. Fold up and repeat behind.
3. Reverse-fold.

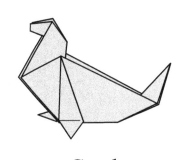

9

Seal

Multibox

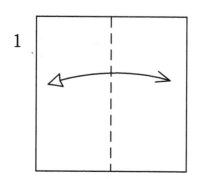

1

Fold and unfold.

2

Fold to the center.

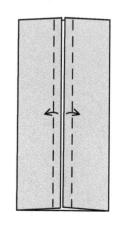

3

Fold thin strips.

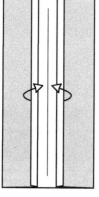

4

Unfold.

5

Fold to the creases.

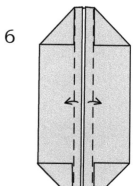

6

Fold along the creases.

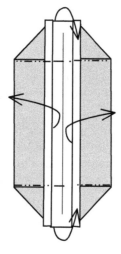

7

Open the box.

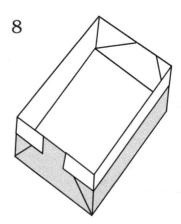

8

Multibox

Box with Lid

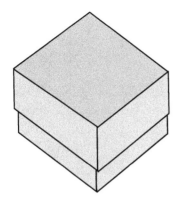

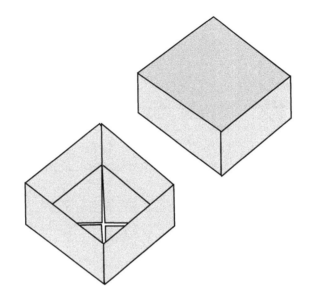

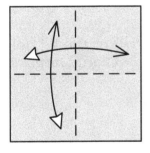

1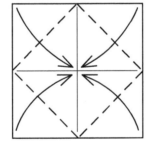

Fold and unfold.

2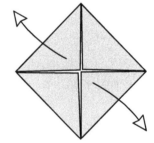

Fold the corners
to the center.

3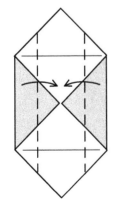

Unfold and rotate.

4

Fold to the center.

5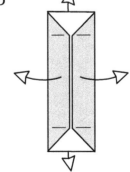

Fold behind.

6

Unfold.

7

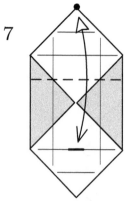

Fold and unfold.

8

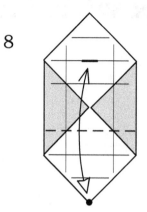

Fold and unfold.

9

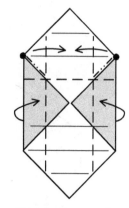

Fold along the creases. The dots will meet.

10

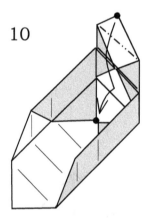

Cover the bottom. The dots will meet.

11

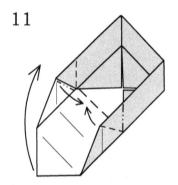

Repeat steps 9–10 in the other direction.

12

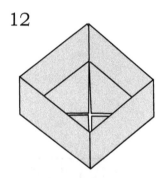

For the lid, fold a slighly larger box.

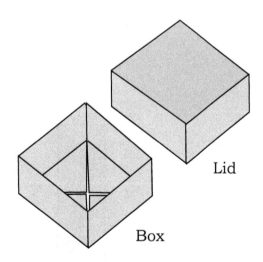

Lid

Box

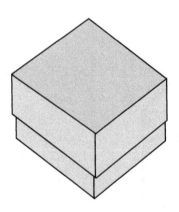

Box with Lid

Gift Box

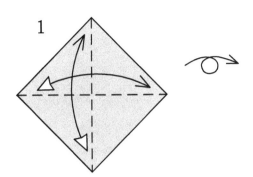

1

Fold and unfold.

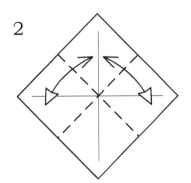

2

Fold and unfold.

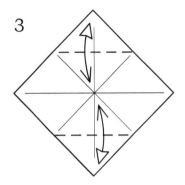

3

Fold and unfold
opposite corners
to the center.

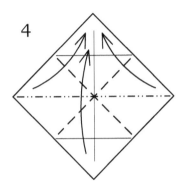

4

Refold along
the creases.

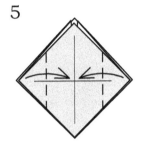

5

Fold to the center.
Repeat behind.

6

Fold to the center.
Repeat behind.

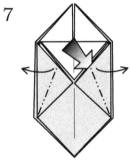

7

Squash folds.
Repeat behind.

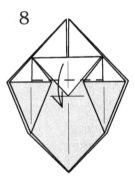

8

Fold down.
Repeat behind.

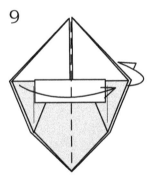

9

Fold the top left
flap to the right
and repeat behind.

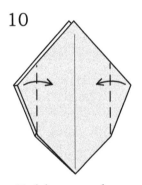

10

Fold towards
the center.
Repeat behind.

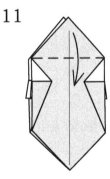

11

Fold down.
Repeat behind.

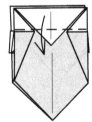

12

Fold down.
Repeat behind.

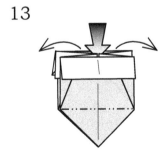

13

Open.

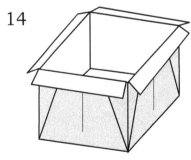

14

Gift Box

Candy Dish

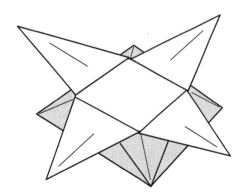

1

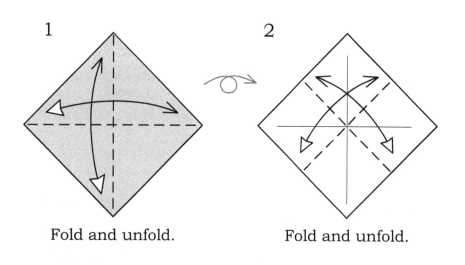

Fold and unfold.

2

Fold and unfold.

3

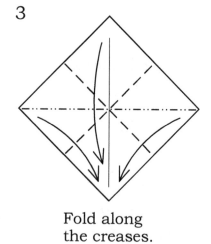

Fold along
the creases.

4

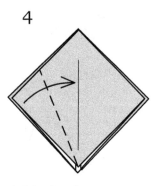

This is the
Preliminary Fold.

5

Squash-fold.

6

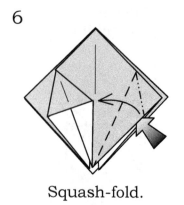

Squash-fold.

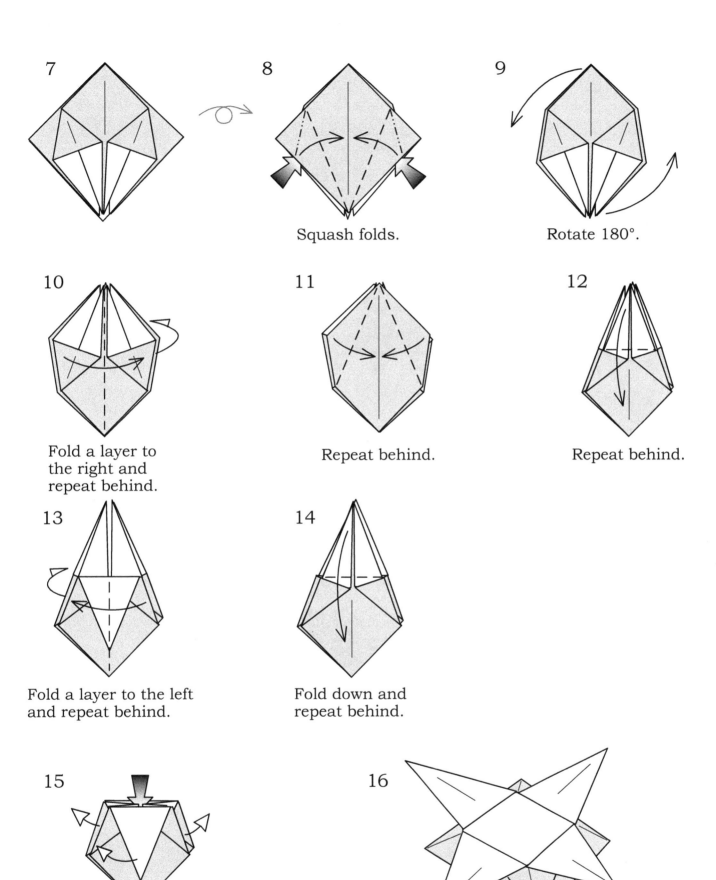

7

8

Squash folds.

9

Rotate 180°.

10

Fold a layer to
the right and
repeat behind.

11

Repeat behind.

12

Repeat behind.

13

Fold a layer to the left
and repeat behind.

14

Fold down and
repeat behind.

15

Open and flatten
the bottom.

16

Candy Dish

CPSIA information can be obtained
at www.ICGtesting.com
Printed in the USA
LVHW020844170520
655785LV00011B/567